This book is dedicated to my children - Mikey, Kobe, and Jojo.

Copyright © 2024 Grow Grit Press LLC. All rights reserved. No part of this book may be reproduced in any form without permission in writing from the publisher. Please send bulk order requests to info@ninjalifehacks.tv

Paperback ISBN: 979-8-89614-018-4
Hardcover ISBN: 979-8-89614-020-7
eBook ISBN: 979-8-89614-019-1

Printed and bound in the USA.
NinjaLifeHacks.tv

Ninja Life Hacks
by Mary Nhin

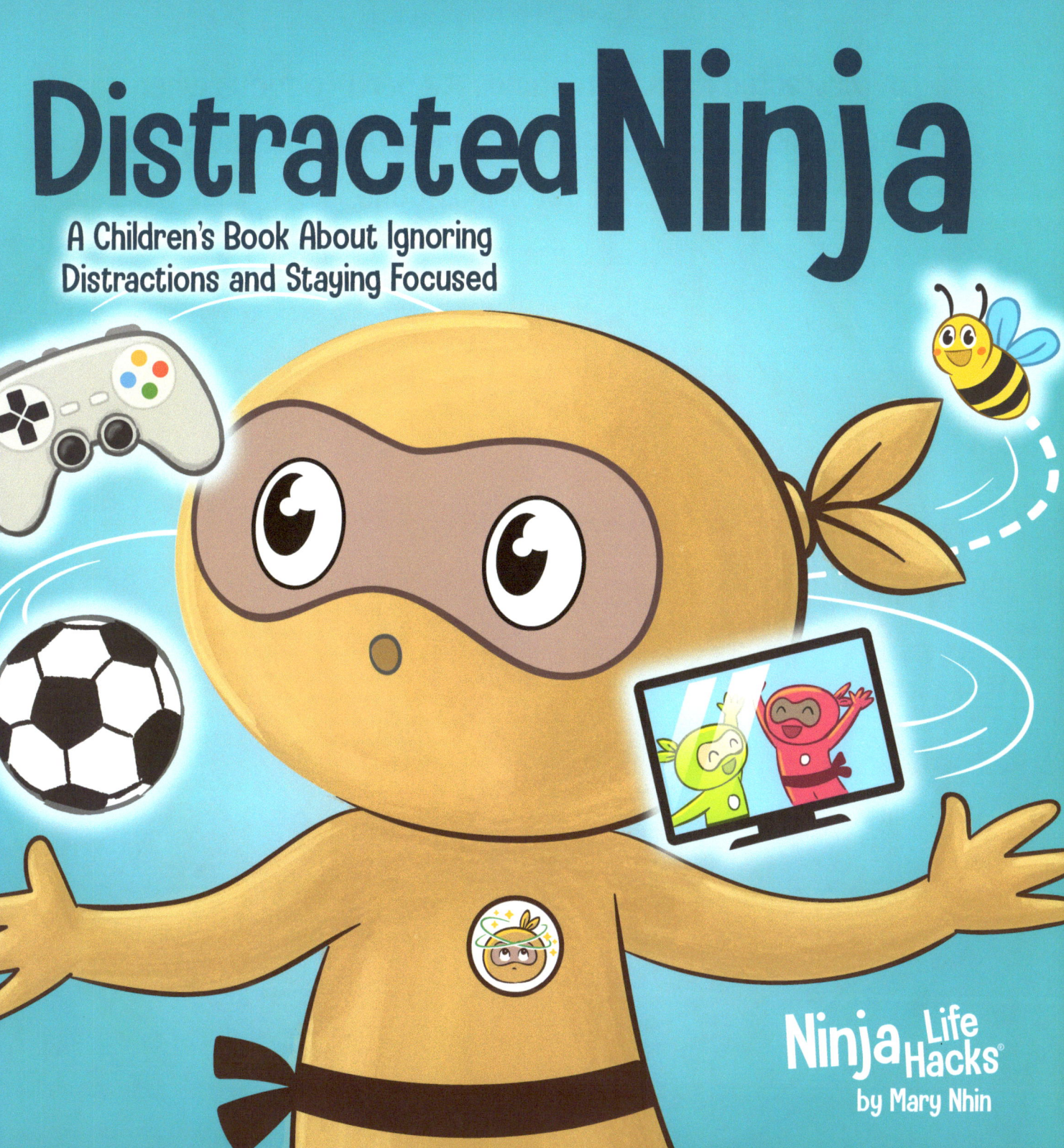

D.O.I.T. Strategy

- **D**: Decide what's important. Choose what you need to focus on right now.
- **O**: Organize your time and space. Clear away distractions and make a plan.
- **I**: Ignore interruptions. Stay focused, even when something tries to pull you away.
- **T**: Try Again if you get distracted. It's okay to lose focus–just come back and keep going!

Even when I did get distracted by something, I didn't get upset. I just **tried** again and kept going. Each time, I got better at focusing.

D.O.I.T. Strategy

- **D**
- **O**
- **I**
- **T**

Check out the fun Distracted Ninja lesson plans at ninjalifehacks.tv

I love to hear from my readers. Email me your feedback or thoughts on what my next story should be at info@ninjalifehacks.tv   Yours truly, Mary

 @marynhin   @GrowGrit
#NinjaLifeHacks

 Ninja Life Hacks

 Mary Nhin   Ninja Life Hacks

 @officialninjalifehacks